WHITE HOUSE
WINNERS

WHAT YOU DON'T KNOW ABOUT THE PRESIDENTS

L. J. TRACOSAS

ILLUSTRATIONS BY JOSH LYNCH

Scholastic Inc.

Of course the president of the United States has a serious job, full of big decisions, important meetings, and lots of responsibilities.

Yes, they get to live in the huge, fancy White House. They travel the world, attend big parties, and are on TV all the time. Some of them even appear on our money!

But what does the president actually *do*? He or she makes up the executive branch of the government, along with his or her staff, working with the other branches of government to make and carry out laws. The president alone is responsible for signing laws (making them into rules for the country) or vetoing laws (preventing them from becoming rules).

The president leads the country, represents the United States in the world, and solves problems with leaders from the U.S. and around the world. He or she also holds the title of commander in chief of the military.

Wow, that is a big job!

THREE BRANCHES OF THE FEDERAL GOVERNMENT

Executive branch: the president and his or her staff, which carries out laws

3

Legislative branch: the Congress (the Senate and House of Representatives), which makes laws

Judicial branch: the Supreme Court and other federal courts, which uphold the laws

Presidents Are People, Too

It probably seems like all presidents are super serious. They have lots of responsibilities. But when presidents aren't working, they are just ordinary people. They pull pranks and throw parties and cheer on their favorite sports teams. They collect stamps and cars and animals. They do all the things that regular people do—except they do them in the White House!

TO RUN FOR PRESIDENT, A PERSON MUST . . .
• be at least thirty-five years old
• be born in the United States
• be a current U.S. citizen, and
• have lived in the United States for fourteen years.

Throughout history, presidents have been known for having tons of quirks, odd obsessions, and hilarious habits. Can you imagine a president walking on stilts? Or a president who falls asleep at dinner? What about a president who loves skydiving? Well, believe it or not, those are all true!

Who's most likely to be a professional bowler? Who's the best musician? Who has the biggest sweet tooth? Who's the best student? Find out the winners of each of these wacky awards—and more—here!

George Washington

BEST SMILE

Why isn't George Washington flashing his pearly whites on the one-dollar bill? Well, the nation's first president had poor dental health. It was so bad that he had only one tooth left in his mouth when he took office! Lots of people think that Washington had false teeth made of wood (ouch, splinters). Not true! He actually had many sets of teeth. He had a set made of brass, one from hippopotamus ivory, another from bone, and one had gold metal wire. Bling! Bling!

 RUNNER-UP: Ulysses S. Grant

When he was a general in the Civil War, Ulysses S. Grant once went off to battle carrying nothing but his toothbrush. Now, that's a guy who takes his teeth seriously!

MASSACHUSETTS · UNITED STATES OF AMERICA

John Adams

7

1st PLACE — BEST PEN PAL

John Adams liked to write letters to keep in touch with family and friends. He loved writing to his wife, Abigail, most of all. The two wrote each other more than eleven hundred letters during their relationship. Another famous pen pal of Adams? Thomas Jefferson. The two were frenemies when they ran against each other in the presidential election. But they eventually made up and sent each other plenty of mail. Historians continue to study their letters.

 RUNNER-UP: Thomas Jefferson

Thomas Jefferson also loved writing letters. Some historians estimate he penned more than eighteen thousand letters in his lifetime.

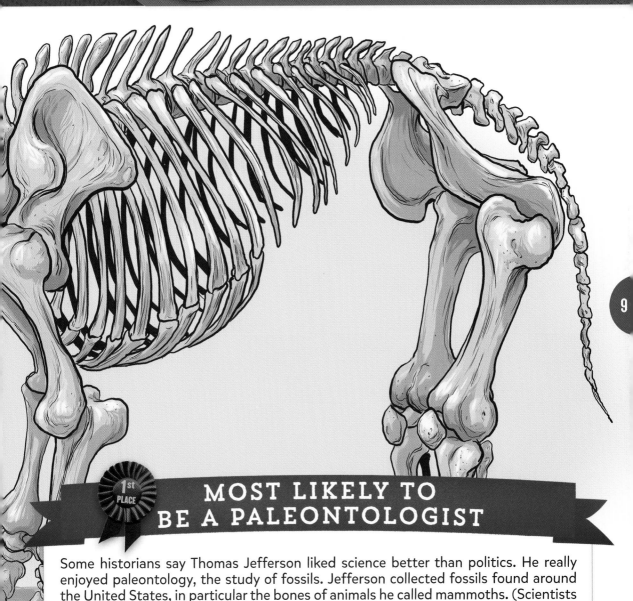

9

1st PLACE
MOST LIKELY TO BE A PALEONTOLOGIST

Some historians say Thomas Jefferson liked science better than politics. He really enjoyed paleontology, the study of fossils. Jefferson collected fossils found around the United States, in particular the bones of animals he called mammoths. (Scientists later found out these were actually mastodons.) These huge early mammals' teeth were each about the size of a fist. Jefferson even tried to put together a mastodon skeleton in the East Room of the White House. Paleontologists have named a fossil after the third president: *Megalonyx jeffersonii* was a giant clawed sloth.

 RUNNER-UP: Barack Obama ★

In 2015, President Barack Obama made Waco Mammoth, a site in Texas that is home to one of the biggest mammoth fossil beds in the country, a national monument.

James Madison

4ᵗʰ President
1809-1817

Hometown:
Port Conway, Virginia

1ˢᵗ PLACE — BIGGEST SWEET TOOTH

James Madison and his wife, Dolley, helped make ice cream one of America's favorite desserts. Creating ice cream back then was tricky because modern refrigerators and freezers hadn't been invented yet. Instead, to keep things cold, you needed huge blocks of ice and an ice house—a whole building that was insulated to keep the winter snow that was packed inside from melting. Dolley served ice cream at her husband's second inaugural ball. What was her favorite flavor? *Oyster* ice cream! (At least the oysters from the nearby Potomac River had a sweet taste!)

★ **RUNNER-UP: Ronald Reagan** ★

Ronald Reagan loved jelly beans, and he celebrated his 1981 inauguration
with three and half *tons* of jelly beans. Now, *that's* a party!

James Monroe

5ᵗʰ President
1817–1825

Hometown:
Westmoreland County, Virginia

1ˢᵗ PLACE

BEST RETRO STYLE

James Monroe was known for his revolutionary fashion—Revolutionary War fashion, that is. By the time Monroe was president, men were wearing pantaloons and top hats. But Monroe put on a powdered wig, knee breeches, silk stockings, and a tricorn hat. In fact, he was the last president to wear one of these triangle-brimmed caps, earning him the nickname "the Last Cocked Hat." His retro style looked totally old-school cool.

 RUNNER-UP: Jimmy Carter

Jimmy Carter was a peanut farmer before getting involved in politics, so he was used to dressing casual. He wore his beige cardigan sweater to dinner and for his TV addresses!

John Quincy Adams

6th President
1825–1829

Hometown:
Braintree, Massachusetts

BEST PROFILE PIC

Say cheese! John Quincy Adams may not have been the first president ever photographed, but his picture is the oldest surviving photo of a U.S. president—even though the photo was taken years after he'd left office. The image was snapped on August 1, 1843, in upstate New York. Four daguerreotypes (*da·gear·o·types*), or old photos made on silver plates instead of paper, were created of Adams that day, all of which he said were "hideous."

 RUNNER-UP: William Henry Harrison

William Henry Harrison was actually the first president to have his photo taken.
He posed on March 4, 1841. But unfortunately the picture was lost.

12

Andrew Jackson

7ᵀᴴ President
1829–1837

Hometown:
Waxhaw settlement, the border
between North and South Carolina

NORTH CAROLINA
UNITED STATES OF AMERICA

1ST PLACE

BIGGEST JOKER

Young Andrew Jackson was famous for his carefree nature and his practical jokes. People called him a "mischievous fellow" and "head of all the rowdies." In one famous prank, Jackson decided to move people's outhouses—outdoor bathrooms like Porta Potties. While everyone was inside the building, Jackson moved the outhouses to new locations that were unknown to everyone else. So when people needed to go, they couldn't find any bathrooms!

 RUNNER-UP: Bill Clinton

According to press reports, when he was leaving office, President Bill Clinton's staff allegedly removed the letter *W* from all of the White House keyboards, so President George W. Bush's staff members couldn't type his middle initial.

13

NEW YORK · UNITED STATES OF AMERICA

Martin Van Buren

14

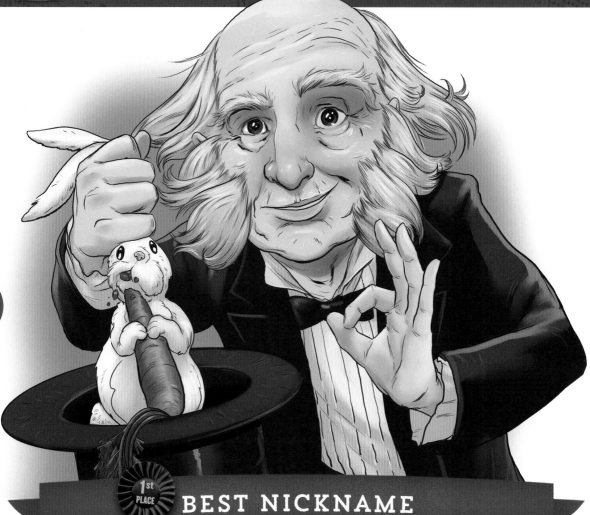

1st PLACE

BEST NICKNAME

Martin Van Buren was a man of many nicknames. Being slim and five feet six inches tall, he was sometimes called "the Little Magician" for his size and political skills. He was also called "the Sly Fox" and "Old Kinderhook," after his birthplace in New York. Van Buren's Old Kinderhook nickname may have inspired one of the words we use today. His supporters formed the "OK Club" to show how much they liked their candidate. Shortly after this, the use of the term OK became wildly popular.

 RUNNER-UP: Ulysses S. Grant

Ulysses S. Grant had so many victories on Civil War battlefields that people said his initials *U* and *S* actually stood for "Unconditional Surrender." He was also known as the "Great Hammerer."

VIRGINIA · UNITED STATES OF AMERICA

William Henry Harrison

9th President
March 1841–April 1841

Hometown:
Charles City County, Virginia

15

1st PLACE BIGGEST BLABBERMOUTH

National war hero William Henry Harrison was a Whig party member with something to say! After winning the 1841 presidential election, Harrison stepped up to the podium and gave the country's longest inaugural address. The speech was timed at more than ninety minutes and was made up of almost nine thousand words. Sadly, some think it was during this long speech, given in bad weather, that Harrison got the pneumonia that may have led to his death thirty-two days later.

 RUNNER-UP: Martin Van Buren

Martin Van Buren could give speeches not only in English but also in Dutch. That's because his hometown, Kinderhook, New York, was formed by Dutch settlers who still spoke the language of their home country. Van Buren is the only president whose first language wasn't English.

John Tyler

10th President
1841–1845

Hometown:
Charles City County, Virginia

1st PLACE · BIGGEST PARTY ANIMAL

Even though John Tyler was a member of the Whig Party, his politics didn't really fit in with the rest of his party's ideas. That's why Whig leader Henry Clay called Tyler "a man without a party." Tyler's wife, Julia, couldn't bear how upset Tyler was. So she decided she'd give her husband the biggest party she could. In February 1845, she hosted an unforgettable shindig at the White House. When someone told Tyler what a great bash it was, he said, "Yes, they cannot say now that I am a president without a party!"

 RUNNER-UP: Andrew Jackson

In 1829, when Andrew Jackson won the election, people could visit the White House to party with the president on his first day in office! His inaugural party is considered the wildest bash the White House has ever seen.

17

1st PLACE — MOST SERIOUS

James K. Polk grew up in a strict and religious Presbyterian community, an influence many historians say was partly responsible for his strong work ethic. His wife was also a very religious woman. Their beliefs meant there could be no alcohol, no dancing, and no card games in the White House. That made for some tame—even lame—presidential gatherings. When Polk was elected, they actually stopped dancing during the inaugural ball while the Polks were in the room. Dancing started up again as soon as they left.

 RUNNER-UP: Calvin Coolidge

Calvin Coolidge was a serious guy—so serious that he even wore a formal hat while shaving! (He said it was to keep his hair out of his eyes.)

Zachary Taylor

12th President
1849–1850

Hometown:
Louisville, Kentucky

🎖 MOST HUMBLE

Zachary Taylor was a war hero. He earned the nickname "Old Rough and Ready" for his success on the battlefields during the War of 1812, the Black Hawk War, and the Second Seminole War. But his great success never went to his head. Even though he was a general, Taylor never wore his uniform or anything that hinted at his rank. One day, while he was visiting soldiers in the field, an officer offered him his trunk to sit on and apologized that it was in such bad shape. Taylor reportedly said, "All I am afraid of is that I will spoil the trunk." What a nice guy!

 RUNNER-UP: George Washington

George Washington stepped down after two terms, even though he was very popular. This humble man said that when he looked back at his administration, he couldn't think of anything he had done wrong on purpose. But he was sensible enough to know that he probably made some mistakes.

OHIO

UNITED STATES OF AMERICA

27th President
1909-1913

Hometown:
Cincinnati, Ohio

35

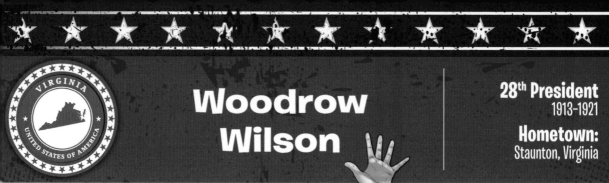

Woodrow Wilson

VIRGINIA · UNITED STATES OF AMERICA

28th President
1913–1921

Hometown:
Staunton, Virginia

36

1st PLACE — BEST STUDENT

As a boy growing up in the South, Woodrow Wilson received much of his early schooling at home from his father. The Civil War had interrupted daily life, including education. But Wilson eventually went to college, and then studied law before getting his doctorate, or Ph.D., in political science. He is the only president to have a Ph.D. This "lifelong student" was a professor at a number of universities before becoming president of Princeton. When he was president of the country, folks often called him by his nickname, "the Schoolmaster."

 RUNNER-UP: Lyndon B. Johnson

Lyndon B. Johnson dreamed of becoming a teacher long before he dreamed of becoming president. He didn't have a lot of money growing up, but he was so committed to his own education that he borrowed tuition money to attend college.

Warren G. Harding

29th President
1921-1923
Hometown:
Corsica, Ohio

1st PLACE — MOST FRIENDLY

Warren G. Harding was known as being a people person. "I love to meet people. It's really the most pleasant thing I do and is really the only fun I have," he said. Rather than going out and giving speeches to large crowds while campaigning, he had visitors come to his home in Marion, Ohio, so he could speak to them in smaller groups. People loved him, too. He won his presidential election by the biggest numbers at the time, and he remained very popular while in office.

 RUNNER-UP: Gerald Ford

President Gerald Ford's kind demeanor and clean-cut image earned him the nickname "Mr. Nice Guy."

Calvin Coolidge

30th President
1923–1929

Hometown:
Plymouth Notch, Vermont

38

1st PLACE — BIGGEST WALLFLOWER

Calvin Coolidge's nickname was "Silent Cal" thanks to his quiet, serious nature. According to one famous story, a woman at a White House dinner party told Coolidge she had made a bet with a friend that she could get at least three words out of him. He didn't even meet her stare when he replied: "You lose." Despite not being talkative, his voice reached thousands of people. His address to Congress after the death of Warren G. Harding was the first presidential speech broadcast over radio.

 RUNNER-UP: Thomas Jefferson

Thomas Jefferson tried to avoid giving speeches as much as possible because of his shyness. He was even known as "the silent member" in Congress while writing the Declaration of Independence.

Herbert Hoover

31st President
1929–1933

Hometown:
West Branch, Iowa

39

 BIGGEST DO-GOODER

Even though his presidency coincided with the Great Depression, which created lots of misfortune for Americans, Hoover was known as "the great humanitarian" for all his good deeds. Before becoming president, he rescued children during the Boxer Rebellion in China. He also led a committee that helped more than 120,000 Americans get home from Europe safely after World War I began. He raised billions of dollars for starving Europeans, and in his retirement, he cofounded the charity organization known as UNICEF.

★ **RUNNER-UP:** Barack Obama ★

President Barack Obama received the Nobel Peace Prize in 2009 for his good work in diplomacy, or keeping good relationships between countries. With the prize, he received $1.4 million, all of which he donated to charity.

Franklin D. Roosevelt

32nd President
1933-1945

Hometown:
Hyde Park, New York

1st PLACE

BIGGEST COLLECTOR

Franklin D. Roosevelt was a stamp collector from the age of eight, and his passion for stamps grew as he got older. He made time every day to organize his collection. He often spent the last thirty minutes of each day looking at his stamps, a habit that relaxed him and got him ready to sleep. FDR even asked the State Department to send over the envelopes they received so he could check out the stamps! He also approved more than two hundred stamps during his time in office and designed some himself.

★ **RUNNER-UP:** Theodore Roosevelt ★

Theodore Roosevelt helped establish the collection for the National Museum of Natural History. During an expedition in Africa, he collected eleven hundred animal specimens.

Harry S. Truman

41

1st PLACE — MOST LIKELY TO SPEAK HIS MIND

If Harry Truman had something to say, he usually didn't hold back—whether it was nice or not. Once, when he was asked about someone whom he disagreed with, Truman said he didn't think the man could even be a dogcatcher. And when a newspaper music critic gave his daughter's singing recital a poor review, Truman sent him a nasty letter saying, among other things, "I never met you, but if I do you'll need a new nose."

 RUNNER-UP: Lyndon B. Johnson

Lyndon B. Johnson always told it like it was. He famously spoke his mind and said that being president was like being a donkey in a hailstorm: "You just have to stand there and take it."

42

34th President
1953–1961

Hometown:
Denison, Texas

43

 MOST LIKELY TO GET A HOLE-IN-ONE

1st PLACE

Golfing is a common presidential pastime. But Dwight D. Eisenhower spent more days on the green than any other president. Records show that Eisenhower played golf on more than one thousand days during his two terms as president. He loved it so much, he installed a putting green at the White House. Eisenhower was always trying to improve his game, and once said that if he didn't, he would "pass a law that no one can ask [him his] golf score." Yes, sir!

 RUNNER-UP: Ronald Reagan

Though President Ronald Reagan didn't golf as much as President Eisenhower, he was probably the first president to putt on a plane.

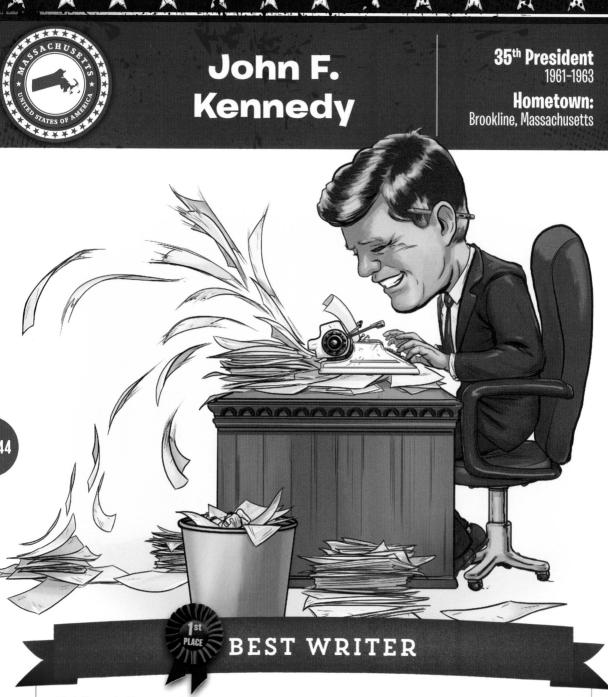

John F. Kennedy

35th President
1961–1963

Hometown:
Brookline, Massachusetts

MASSACHUSETTS · UNITED STATES OF AMERICA

44

1st PLACE

BEST WRITER

Childhood illnesses kept John F. Kennedy in bed for long stretches. He passed the time with stacks of books. Some of his favorite books were spy novels. He particularly loved Ian Fleming's super-spy James Bond series. Kennedy loved them so much that he even tried writing a spy novel himself! It was never published, but Kennedy did write a book of essays, *Profiles in Courage*, about eight congressmen whom he thought were brave in difficult times. The book won him a Pulitzer Prize, an award for great writing. He's the only president to claim that honor.

★ **RUNNER-UP:** Abraham Lincoln ★

Although Abraham Lincoln didn't write a novel, his letters and speeches have been collected in many books. During his lifetime, Lincoln was famous for his storytelling and for his jokes, which kept crowds entertained during his speeches.

Lyndon B. Johnson

TEXAS
UNITED STATES OF AMERICA

45

1st PLACE — WILDEST WHEELS

Lyndon B. Johnson loved cars! He had a small collection of them at his Texas ranch. In the garage were Lincoln Continental convertibles, a 1915 fire truck, and a 1934 Volkswagen Phaeton, as well as a special vehicle—an Amphicar, the first amphibious car that could drive on land *and* in the water available for citizens to buy. Johnson liked to take visitors for a ride around his ranch and pretend to lose control near the lake. Just when his visitors expected to crash into the water, the car would float and they'd go for a sail.

 RUNNER-UP: William McKinley

William McKinley was the first president to ride in a car. He took a quick spin in a Stanley Steamer, an early vehicle powered by steam rather than gas.

Richard Nixon

46

 MOST LIKELY TO BE A PROFESSIONAL BOWLER

Richard Nixon was a pretty good bowler—he rolled a high score of 232 out of a possible 300 points. Nixon's wife, Patricia, also enjoyed the sport, and together they built a one-lane alley in the White House basement. It wasn't the first alley in the White House. A two-lane alley had been installed for President Truman, but he didn't use it much. Nixon, on the other hand, often bowled alone late at night, practicing and grading his scores.

★ **RUNNER-UP:** George W. Bush ★

President George W. Bush and his family liked to use the Nixon bowling alley. He was also invited to give a speech during a meeting of the Bowling Proprietors' Association of America.

Gerald Ford

38th President
1974–1977

Hometown:
Omaha, Nebraska

47

🎀 1st PLACE BEST LOOKING

As a young college graduate, Gerald Ford was tall, athletic, and handsome, with blond hair and blue eyes. People said he was good-looking enough to be a model. As a matter of fact, Ford *was* a fashion model. He took modeling jobs on the side to make extra money. One of his biggest shoots was for the cover of *Cosmopolitan* magazine, where Ford posed in his navy uniform. He later met his wife, Elizabeth Anne Bloomer, during another modeling job.

 RUNNER-UP: Franklin Pierce

In addition to having great hair, President Franklin Pierce was quite
the looker. One of his nicknames was "Handsome Frank."

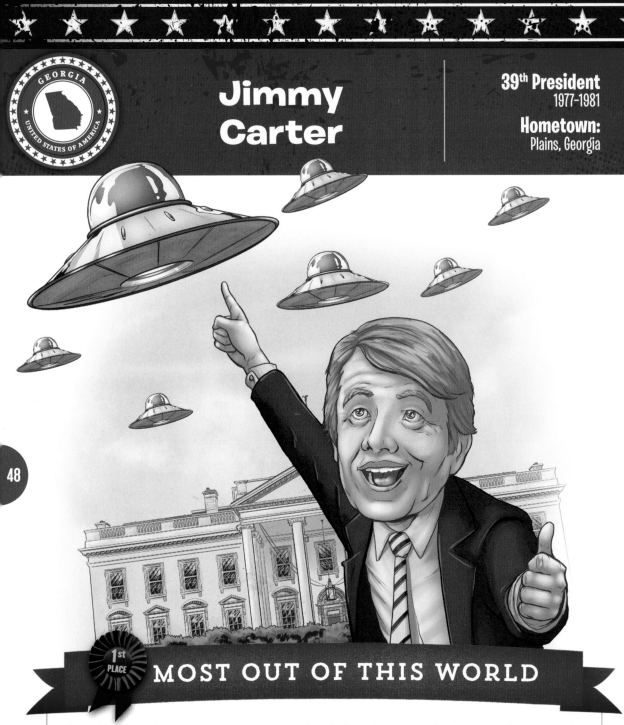

Jimmy Carter

48

1st PLACE — MOST OUT OF THIS WORLD

One day in 1969, Jimmy Carter saw a brightly colored craft hovering in the night sky. It was an unidentified flying object—a UFO! Carter said it was the "darndest thing [he'd] ever seen." Carter and several other people saw the UFO while standing outside before a meeting in Leary, Georgia. The other people with him described it as being the size of the moon. Several years later, as governor of Georgia, Carter submitted a report about his experience with the UFO. Investigations were never able to confirm what the object was.

 RUNNER-UP: Dwight D. Eisenhower

The first president to give the go-ahead for a space mission was Dwight D. Eisenhower in 1955. The mission sent a scientific satellite into orbit. Eisenhower also made important decisions that lead to the creation of the National Aeronautics and Space Administration (NASA) in 1958.

Ronald Reagan

ILLINOIS · UNITED STATES OF AMERICA

40th President
1981–1989

Hometown:
Tampico, Illinois

49

1st PLACE

BIGGEST CELEBRITY

This well-liked president was popular even before being elected. Reagan was a famous sportscaster, movie star, and television star. He even appeared in a movie with a chimpanzee called *Bedtime for Bonzo*. He made fifty-four films in all, and he was on TV for eight years as an actor before appearing on TV again, this time as a politician.

★ **RUNNERS-UP:** John F. Kennedy and Abraham Lincoln ★

National surveys are done every year to find out who Americans think was the best president. Often, the winner is either John F. Kennedy, Abraham Lincoln, or the presidential celeb himself, Ronald Reagan.

George H. W. Bush

41ˢᵗ President
1989-1993

Hometown:
Milton, Massachusetts

1ˢᵗ PLACE

BIGGEST DAREDEVIL

Behind George H. W. Bush's reputation as a kind and gentle man lies a high-flying thrill-seeker! For his seventy-fifth birthday, the former president didn't just celebrate with a nice dinner and birthday cake with family—he jumped out of a plane! He loved skydiving so much, Bush did it again for his eightieth birthday, his eighty-fifth birthday, and again for his ninetieth birthday. In all, his family says he's taken the leap eight times—including his first jump as a sailor, after his plane was shot down in World War II.

★ **RUNNER-UP:** Theodore Roosevelt ★

Theodore Roosevelt loved adventure. He caught an outlaw out west, hunted big game, and was a colonel for the Rough Rider regiment in the Spanish-American War. He also went on an expedition in uncharted lands along the River of Doubt in Brazil.

Millard Fillmore

13th President
1850-1853

Hometown:
Moravia, New York

 1st PLACE

BIGGEST BOOKWORM

This president loved words and books! Wherever he went, Millard Fillmore carried a dictionary with him so he could build his vocab. When he first entered the White House, he was shocked to find it lacking reading material, so he and his wife, Abigail, created the first White House library. In 1851, when a fire flared up at the Library of Congress, Fillmore raced to battle the blaze and save his books. He also sponsored a bill to replace the books damaged in the fire.

★ **RUNNER-UP:** Thomas Jefferson ★

By 1814, Thomas Jefferson had the largest personal library of anyone in the United States, with 6,487 books. He sold his books for $23,950 to create a new Library of Congress after the original one was burned by the British during the War of 1812.

19

NEW HAMPSHIRE · UNITED STATES OF AMERICA

Franklin Pierce

14th President
1853–1857

Hometown:
Hillsborough, New Hampshire

20

1st PLACE

BEST HAIR

Historians consider Franklin Pierce's term as president to be mostly forgettable because things seemed so calm. But what was *not* forgettable about Pierce was his hair. A huge wave of curly black strands rose from the top of his head and was "combed on a deep slant over his wide forehead," according to people who saw him.

 RUNNER-UP: John F. Kennedy

John F. Kennedy was known as a fashionable dresser, but he was also famous for his great hair.
He kept it short at the sides and longer on top, and there never seemed to be a hair out of place.

James Buchanan

15th President
1857–1861

Hometown:
Cove Gap, Pennsylvania

21

 MOST INDEPENDENT

James Buchanan was a handsome man who dressed well and had excellent manners. Still, even though he was charming, James Buchanan was the only president who was never married. When a group of White House visitors noted that everything was perfect except for one thing—there was no lady of the house—Buchanan said, "That is my misfortune, not my fault." Harriet Lane, Buchanan's niece, acted as the First Lady and hosted important events and beautiful parties.

 RUNNER-UP: Grover Cleveland

Grover Cleveland was single when he first entered the White House. He became the only president married at the White House when he and Frances Folsom tied the knot in 1886.

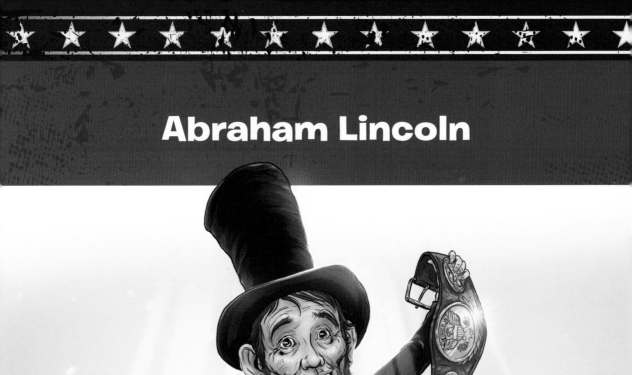

Abraham Lincoln

22

23

1st PLACE

MOST LIKELY TO BE A PROFESSIONAL WRESTLER

At six feet four inches tall, and muscly from farm work, Abraham Lincoln was a tower of power. He pinned his way to a reputation as the best wrestler in his county. He also apparently talked some trash. After easily tossing an opponent out of the ring on the first try, Lincoln reportedly turned to the crowd and challenged anyone to take him on. No one dared. In three hundred bouts, Lincoln had only one recorded loss. You can even find Lincoln in the National Wrestling Hall of Fame.

★ **RUNNER-UP:** George Washington ★

George Washington spent some time in the wrestling ring, too. He was a champion in his county when he was a young teen, and even wrestled competitors at the ripe old age of forty-seven.

Andrew Johnson

17th President
1865–1869

Hometown:
Raleigh, North Carolina

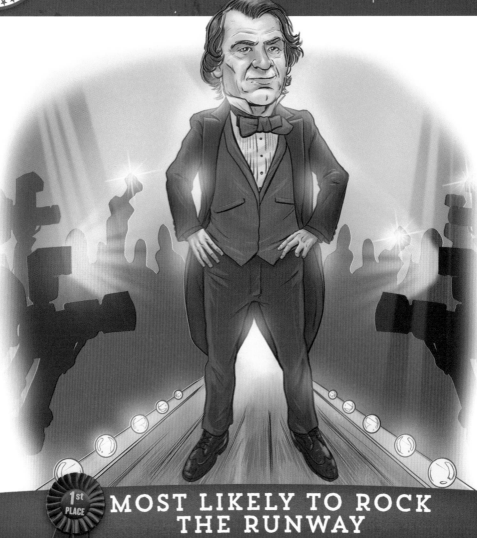

1st PLACE — MOST LIKELY TO ROCK THE RUNWAY

When Andrew Johnson was thirteen years old, he was an apprentice—or student—to a tailor. Johnson was supposed to work there for six years with his brother, but they stayed for only two. Johnson eventually opened up his own tailor shop in Greeneville, Tennessee. During this time, Johnson—who had never gone to school—had his wife and others read aloud to him while he stitched so he could learn more. When he got into politics, he held meetings at his tailor shop. He continued to sew his own suits for the rest of his life, even while he was president!

 RUNNER-UP: George H. W. Bush

Post-presidency, George H. W. Bush has caught the eye of fashionistas everywhere for his bold choice in . . . socks! He wore a hot-pink pair to the opening of his son George W. Bush's presidential library, and even sported some with his smiling face on them at a football game.

Ulysses S. Grant

18th President
1869–1877

Hometown:
Point Pleasant, Ohio

OHIO · UNITED STATES OF AMERICA

25

1ST PLACE

MOST SUPERSTITIOUS

From a very young age, Ulysses S. Grant thought it was bad luck to walk back and retrace his steps. According to stories, even if he accidentally passed a store he was going to, he wouldn't turn around to go back to it. He'd keep going forward and find a new way to get there. This, of course, served him well in the Civil War. Because he never retraced his steps, he succeeded in battle where others had failed. Grant wouldn't retreat and was always looking for new ways to achieve his goals.

 RUNNER-UP: Franklin D. Roosevelt

President Franklin D. Roosevelt had triskaidekaphobia (*tri·sky·dek·uh·fo·be·uh*)—a fear of the number thirteen. Roosevelt wouldn't travel on the thirteenth of the month or dine at a dinner with thirteen guests.

Rutherford B. Hayes

19th President
1877-1881

Hometown:
Delaware, Ohio

Typestyle

1st PLACE — BIGGEST TRENDSETTER

Rutherford B. Hayes was the first president to do lots of neat things. During his term, he was the first president to travel to the West Coast, which he did on a seventy-one-day train tour. You could say he was a techie, too. He had the first telephone installed in the White House in 1878 (the president's phone number was just the number 1!), and he was also the first president to use a typewriter in the White House. He held the first Easter Egg Roll—a tradition still held today—and he was the first person ever to have a Siamese cat in the United States.

 RUNNER-UP: John F. Kennedy

On his inauguration day, President John F. Kennedy was the first president not to wear headwear of any kind during an inaugural event. This almost killed the hat business, because men everywhere suddenly went without hats, just like the president.

James A. Garfield

20th President
March 1881–September 1881

Hometown:
Orange Township, Ohio

1st PLACE — MOST HANDY

James A. Garfield was known as a smart man with plenty of skills even before becoming president. He taught school, was a soldier on the battlefield, and worked hard in Congress. But he was very well known for another handy skill: being ambidextrous (*am·be·dek·struss*). That means he could use both hands equally, even when he was writing. Garfield had even more handy tricks up his sleeve. He had studied languages in school, so he could write ancient Greek with one hand and Latin with the other *at the same time*!

 RUNNER-UP: Gerald Ford

President Ford was also ambidextrous, but it came with a catch! He was left-handed only when he was sitting down; if he was on his feet, he was right-handed. Photos of President Ford show him writing with his left hand at his desk, but throwing a football with his right hand during games.

Chester A. Arthur

🏆 BEST DRESSED

President Arthur was nicknamed "The Gentleman Boss" and "Elegant Arthur" for his style and large wardrobe. He wore a different outfit for every event. Sometimes that meant he changed clothes several times a day. He reportedly owned eighty pairs of pants. President Arthur's impressive style wasn't limited to his clothes. His mutton chop facial hair was quite the "in" style for the 1880s.

 RUNNER-UP: Harry S. Truman

President Truman owned a haberdashery, or men's clothing store, in Kansas City before he became president. And he always made appearances in a coat and tie.

Grover Cleveland

22nd President
1885–1889

Hometown:
Caldwell, New Jersey

29

1st PLACE — BEST COMEBACK

Grover Cleveland was said to have laser-like focus on whatever was in front of him during his presidencies. That's right—*presidencies*. Cleveland is the only person to serve two nonconsecutive terms as president.

To be continued . . .

Benjamin Harrison

OHIO · UNITED STATES OF AMERICA

23rd President
1889–1893

Hometown:
North Bend, Ohio

30

1st PLACE

WORST HANDSHAKE

Even though Harrison was a gifted public speaker who could get a crowd fired up with one of his speeches, people who met him in person were left feeling a little . . . cold. Harrison just couldn't warm up to folks one-on-one. This was such a problem that one of his supporters would whisk Harrison away from the public after his speeches. The supporter said, "[He] had the crowd red-hot. I did not want him to freeze it out of them with his hand-shaking." Another person said it was like shaking a "wilted petunia." One of Harrison's nicknames was "the Human Iceberg."

★ **RUNNER-UP:** Gerald Ford ★

In 1975, Gerald Ford tumbled down the steps of Air Force One only to pop right up and thrust out his hand for a shake with the Austrian chancellor!

Grover Cleveland

SEE, I TOLD YOU!

1ST PLACE — BEST COMEBACK

Grover Cleveland is the only person to serve two nonconsecutive terms as president. Cleveland served one term, lost the election the next term, and then won the one after that. Cleveland didn't lose his focus on the presidency after losing the election in 1888. He was back on top again in 1893 for his second go-round.

 RUNNER-UP: Franklin D. Roosevelt

Since George Washington stepped down after two terms, there was an unwritten rule that no president should seek a third term—at least until Franklin D. Roosevelt. He won a third term during World War II in 1940, and then a *fourth* term in 1944.

William McKinley

25th President
1897-1901

Hometown:
Canton, Ohio

🏅 BEST HUSBAND

William McKinley first met Ida Saxton at a church picnic. Two years later, they met again while Ida was working at a bank. They fell deeply in love and married soon after. McKinley's admiration for his wife was well known. When he was governor of Ohio, he would go to an office window and wave in the direction of her hotel every day at three o'clock. He also broke tradition and insisted that Ida sit next to him at state dinners rather than across the table. They were total lovebirds.

 RUNNER-UP: Richard Nixon

It was love at first sight for Richard Nixon when he met his future wife, Pat, during theater auditions. He said he knew that day he would marry her!

Theodore Roosevelt

 1st PLACE

MOST LIKELY TO JOIN THE CIRCUS

President Roosevelt was known for being an outdoorsman, a soldier, a great writer, and a bookworm. He even won the Nobel Peace Prize. But during his presidency, the White House was never quiet. His six children had many, many pets: five bears, a lizard, a pig, a badger, a parrot, five guinea pigs, a hen, a rooster, a hyena, an owl, a rabbit, a snake, a rat, a pony, twelve horses, a squirrel, a raccoon, a coyote, a zebra, four dogs, and two cats. And every member of Teddy Roosevelt's family owned a pair of stilts—even the president!

 RUNNER-UP: Calvin Coolidge ⭐

Although President Coolidge wasn't a stilt walker, he housed a small zoo with twenty-six pets—including two lions, a black bear, and a pygmy hippo.

William Howard Taft

MOST LIKELY TO FALL ASLEEP

1ST PLACE

William Howard Taft was a snore. Really! He was constantly falling asleep. It didn't matter whether he was in a meeting, at an important presidential dinner, attending a fancy opera, or a church service. He even fell asleep during funerals. His wife, Nellie, nicknamed him "Sleeping Beauty." Taft wasn't just tuckered out from his presidential duties. He actually had a condition called sleep apnea, which made it hard for him to sleep for long periods of time without waking up. Because of this, he was always tired.

★ **RUNNER-UP:** George W. Bush ★

George W. Bush fancied a midday snooze. He even told reporters one day that after he finished answering their questions he was going to "head on home and have a nap."

Bill Clinton

42nd President
1993-2001

Hometown:
Hope, Arkansas

1st PLACE — MOST MUSICAL

Bill Clinton was an excellent saxophone player in high school. He even made first chair in the Arkansas state band. But despite how much he rocked the tenor sax, the call to public service moved him more. On a trip to Washington, D.C., then-sixteen-year-old Clinton met President John F. Kennedy. Clinton decided right then that he would put down his sax and take up politics. He did continue to play for fun, though, even appearing on *The Arsenio Hall Show* in cool shades to blow the song "Heartbreak Hotel" with the late-night band.

 RUNNER-UP: Richard Nixon

Nixon's mom made him take piano lessons when he was growing up, and they paid off! While he was president, Nixon played during events at the White House and at the Grand Ole Opry, a famous country music concert hall in Tennessee. He also played the saxophone, clarinet, accordion, and violin.

George W. Bush

43rd President
2001-2009

Hometown:
New Haven, Connecticut

CONNECTICUT · UNITED STATES OF AMERICA

1st PLACE · MOST SCHOOL SPIRIT

George W. Bush has always had patriotic spirit, but growing up he had team spirit, too. Bush was head cheerleader at his high school, Phillips Academy, in Massachusetts. He not only cheered on the school's sports teams, he also cheered up his fellow classmates. The dean at his academy said that Bush had "raised school spirit to its highest level" in decades. In addition to his cheerleading duties, Bush created weekly skits and funny pep talks that he delivered at school assemblies.

 RUNNERS-UP: Dwight D. Eisenhower and Ronald Reagan

After an injury benched him for football, Eisenhower supported his team at West Point by cheerleading.
In Illinois, Reagan also cheered on athletes at Eureka College as a member of the cheer squad.

Barack Obama

1st PLACE BIGGEST SPORTS FAN

Barack Obama's nickname in high school was "Barry O'Bomber" because he was so good at shooting hoops, and he still loves to play. He even converted the indoor tennis court at the White House so he could play a full-court game of hoops inside. But Obama isn't just a B-ball fan. He likes playing—and watching—all kinds of sports. He's a big fan of his hometown baseball team the Chicago White Sox. In fact, after a perfect game, Obama called the team's pitcher to congratulate him on an "extraordinary achievement."

 RUNNER-UP: Gerald Ford

You couldn't keep young Gerald Ford from the field (or pool, or track, or court). He loved sports. He was on two championship football teams at the University of Michigan and was a team MVP. He also loved swimming, running, and playing tennis.

54

45th President:
2017-Present

Hometown:
New York, New York

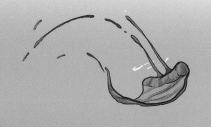

1st PLACE · STRANGEST EATER

New Yorkers are famous for loving their pizza, and Donald Trump is no exception. But very, very unlike other New Yorkers—and most everyone else, for that matter— he never eats a whole slice. He doesn't like to eat the dough. Trump scrapes all the toppings off of the pie—the cheese, peppers, pepperoni, even the sauce—so he doesn't have to eat the crust or base. Why? He wants to avoid the extra calories.

 RUNNERS-UP: James Garfield and William Henry Harrison

Believe it or not, squirrel stew was the favorite food of not one but two presidents. James Garfield couldn't get enough of the stuff. And William Henry Harrison loved it so much that he even served it to supporters on the campaign trail.

The most well-known house in the country is at 1600 Pennsylvania Avenue in Washington, D.C. Behind those famous front doors, there are:

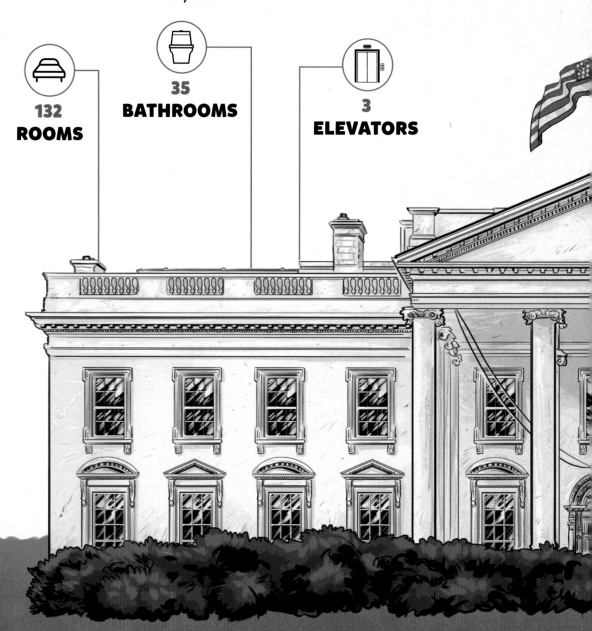

132
ROOMS

35
BATHROOMS

3
ELEVATORS

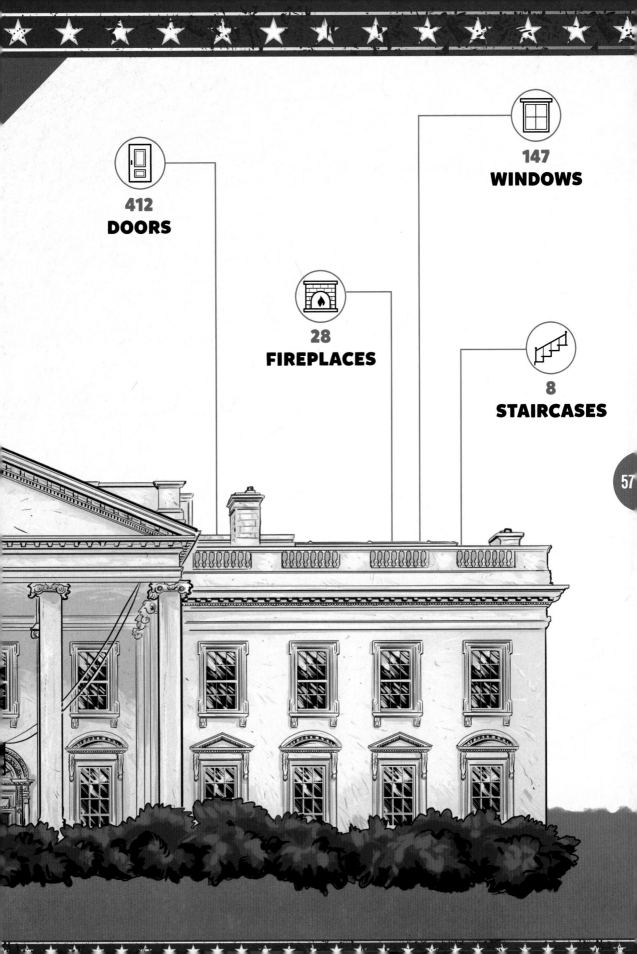

412 DOORS

147 WINDOWS

28 FIREPLACES

8 STAIRCASES

White House Timeline

1789
People begin to talk about building an official President's House near the Potomac River. James Hoban, an Irish-born architect, wins a competition to design the residence.

1792
Building begins on the President's House and continues for eight years. It was made from sandstone.

1798
The President's House is painted with a protective white lime-based coating, giving the house its trademark look. It was nicknamed "the White House" by people who lived in the area.

1901
Theodore Roosevelt decides to make the White House the official name of the presidential home.

1877
President Rutherford B. Hayes installs the first telephone in the White House. It's phone number? Just 1!

1909
William Taft adds on to the executive wing of the residence, creating the Oval Office—a special office for the president.

1913
Woodrow Wilson's wife, Ellen, creates the Rose Garden, which is eventually used as the setting for outdoor press conferences.

1929
A fire in the executive wing leads to more construction that continues through the 1930s. During this time, the executive wing gets renamed the West Wing, and a swimming pool is added.

2009
Barack Obama alters the White House tennis court so it can double as a full-court indoor basketball court.

1992
George H. W. Bush wires the White House for the Internet.

1800

John and Abigail Adams are the first to move in, even though construction had not finished yet.

1805

Thomas Jefferson makes some renovations, including adding early bathrooms called water closets. He allows citizens to tour the home on New Year's Day and July 4th.

1814

The British burn the President's House to the ground during the War of 1812. Architect James Hoban is asked to rebuild the entire thing again—and he does. President James Madison and his wife, Dolley, know it is important that the symbolic house be rebuilt just as it was before it was destroyed.

1829

The North Portico is added.

1824

The South Portico—or columned entrance—is added.

1817

James and Dolley Madison move into the reconstructed President's House. They bring their fancy French furniture and decorations.

1942

A movie theater is added to the East Wing.

1945–1952

Major interior reconstruction and redesign happens during the Truman administration to address structural issues. During this time, Truman also puts the first TV set in the White House.

1947

The White House staff constructs the building's first bowling alley as a birthday gift for Harry Truman—but Truman didn't like bowling!

1978

Jimmy Carter brings the first computer and laser printer to the White House.

1969

Richard Nixon builds a second one-lane bowling alley in the basement of the White House.

1961

John F. Kennedy creates the Situation Room, where all defense organizations send information 24/7, so the president is never left out of the loop.

Presidential Hometown Map

WEST

37. Richard Nixon
Yorba Linda, California

North Dakota

Minnesota

South Dakota

Wisconsin

Washington

Montana

Oregon

Idaho

Wyoming

Nebraska

Iowa

(31)

(40)

(38)

Illi

(16)

Nevada

Utah

Kansas

Missouri

Colorado

(33)

California

(37)

Arizona

New Mexico

Oklahoma

Arkansas

(34)

(42)

Texas

Mississippi

PACIFIC

44. Barack Obama
Honolulu, Hawaii

(36)

Louisiana

Alaska

(44)

Hawaii

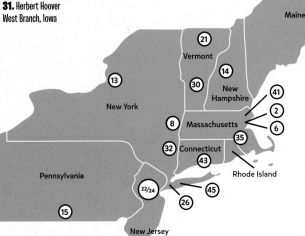

MIDWEST

16. Abraham Lincoln
Springfield, Illinois

18. Ulysses S. Grant
Point Pleasant, Ohio

19. Rutherford B. Hayes
Delaware, Ohio

20. James A. Garfield
Orange Township, Ohio

23. Benjamin Harrison
North Bend, Ohio

25. William McKinley
Canton, Ohio

27. William Howard Taft
Cincinnati, Ohio

29. Warren G. Harding
Corsica, Ohio

31. Herbert Hoover
West Branch, Iowa

33. Harry S. Truman
Lamar, Missouri

38. Gerald Ford
Omaha, Nebraska

40. Ronald Reagan
Tampico, Illinois

NORTHEAST

2. John Adams
Braintree, Massachusetts

6. John Quincy Adams
Braintree, Massachusetts

8. Martin Van Buren
Kinderhook, New York

13. Millard Fillmore
Moravia, New York

14. Franklin Pierce
Hillsborough, New Hampshire

15. James Buchanan
Cove Gap, Pennsylvania

21. Chester A. Arthur
Fairfield, Vermont

22. & 24. Grover Cleveland
Caldwell, New Jersey

26. Theodore Roosevelt
New York, New York

30. Calvin Coolidge
Plymouth Notch, Vermont

32. Franklin D. Roosevelt
Hyde Park, New York

35. John F. Kennedy
Brookline, Massachusetts

41. George H. W. Bush
Milton, Massachusetts

43. George W. Bush
New Haven, Connecticut

45. Donald Trump
New York, New York

SOUTH

1. George Washington
Westmoreland County, Virginia

3. Thomas Jefferson
Shadwell, Virginia

4. James Madison
Port Conway, Virginia

5. James Monroe
Westmoreland County, Virginia

7. Andrew Jackson
Waxhaw settlement, on the border between North and South Carolina

9. William Henry Harrison
Charles City County, Virginia

10. John Tyler
Charles City County, Virginia

11. James K. Polk
Pineville, North Carolina

12. Zachary Taylor
Louisville, Kentucky

17. Andrew Johnson
Raleigh, North Carolina

28. Woodrow Wilson
Staunton, Virginia

34. Dwight D. Eisenhower
Denison, Texas

36. Lyndon B. Johnson
Stonewall, Texas

39. Jimmy Carter
Plains, Georgia

42. Bill Clinton
Hope, Arkansas

Presidents of the United States

George Washington
1st President
Birth: 1732; Death: 1799
No political parties

John Adams
2nd President
Birth: 1735; Death: 1826
Federalist Party

Thomas Jefferson
3rd President
Birth: 1743; Death: 1826
Democratic-Republican Party

James Madison
4th President
Birth: 1751; Death: 1836
Democratic-Republican Party

James Monroe
5th President
Birth: 1758; Death: 1831
Democratic-Republican Party

John Quincy Adams
6th President
Birth: 1767; Death: 1848
Democratic-Republican Party

Andrew Jackson
7th President
Birth: 1767; Death: 1845
Democratic Party

Martin Van Buren
8th President
Birth: 1782; Death: 1862
Democratic Party

William Henry Harrison
9th President
Birth: 1773; Death: 1841
Whig Party

John Tyler
10th President
Birth: 1790; Death: 1862
Whig Party

James K. Polk
11th President
Birth: 1795; Death: 1849
Democratic Party

Zachary Taylor
12th President
Birth: 1784; Death: 1850
Whig Party

Millard Fillmore
13th President
Birth: 1800; Death: 1874
Whig Party

Franklin Pierce
14th President
Birth: 1804; Death: 1869
Democratic Party

James Buchanan
15th President
Birth: 1791; Death: 1868
Democratic Party

Abraham Lincoln
16th President
Birth: 1809; Death: 1865
Republican Party

Andrew Johnson
17th President
Birth: 1808; Death: 1875
Democratic Party

Ulysses S. Grant
18th President
Birth: 1822; Death: 1885
Republican Party

Rutherford B. Hayes
19th President
Birth: 1822; Death: 1893
Republican Party

James A. Garfield
20th President
Birth: 1831; Death: 1881
Republican Party

Chester A. Arthur
21st President
Birth: 1829; Death: 1886
Republican Party

Grover Cleveland
22nd President
Birth: 1837; Death: 1908
Democratic Party

Benjamin Harrison
23rd President
Birth: 1833; Death: 1901
Republican Party

John F. Kennedy
35th President
Birth: 1917; Death: 1963
Democratic Party

Grover Cleveland
24th President
Birth: 1837; Death: 1908
Democratic Party

Lyndon B. Johnson
36th President
Birth: 1908; Death: 1973
Democratic Party

William McKinley
25th President
Birth: 1843; Death: 1901
Republican Party

Richard Nixon
37th President
Birth: 1913; Death: 1994
Republican Party

Theodore Roosevelt
26th President
Birth: 1858; Death: 1919
Republican Party

Gerald Ford
38th President
Birth: 1913; Death: 2006
Republican Party

William Howard Taft
27th President
Birth: 1857; Death: 1930
Republican Party

Jimmy Carter
39th President
Birth: 1924
Democratic Party

Woodrow Wilson
28th President
Birth: 1856; Death: 1924
Democratic Party

Ronald Reagan
40th President
Birth: 1911; Death: 2004
Republican Party

Warren G. Harding
29th President
Birth: 1865; Death: 1923
Republican Party

George H. W. Bush
41st President
Birth: 1924
Republican Party

63

Calvin Coolidge
30th President
Birth: 1872; Death: 1933
Republican Party

Bill Clinton
42nd President
Birth: 1946
Democratic Party

Herbert Hoover
31st President
Birth: 1874; Death: 1964
Republican Party

George W. Bush
43rd President
Birth: 1946
Republican Party

Franklin D. Roosevelt
32nd President
Birth: 1882; Death: 1945
Democratic Party

Barack Obama
44th President
Birth: 1961
Democratic Party

Harry S. Truman
33rd President
Birth: 1884; Death: 1972
Democratic Party

Donald Trump
45th President
Birth: 1946
Republican Party

Dwight D. Eisenhower
34th President
Birth: 1890; Death: 1969
Republican Party

Index

ISBN 978-1-338-12997-7
ISBN 978-1-338-15978-3

10 9 8 7 6 5 4 3 2 1   17 18 19 20 21

Printed in the U.S.A.   88
First edition, January 2017

Book produced by becker&mayer
A division of Quarto Group US Inc.